SCHIRMER'S LIBRARY
OF MUSICAL CLASSICS

Vol. 1767

GEORG PHILIPP TELEMANN

Four Sonatas
For Flute and Piano

Edited by
MILTON WITTGENSTEIN

Figured bass realization by
THOMAS WILT

G. SCHIRMER, Inc.

DISTRIBUTED BY

HAL•LEONARD®
CORPORATION
7777 W. BLUEMOUND RD. P.O. BOX 13819 MILWAUKEE, WI 53213

Sonata in G major
for Flute and Piano

Georg Philipp Telemann (1681-1767)
Edited by Milton Wittgenstein
Figured bass realization by Thomas Wilt

42805Cx

Allegro ♩= 108

Allegro ♩ = 138

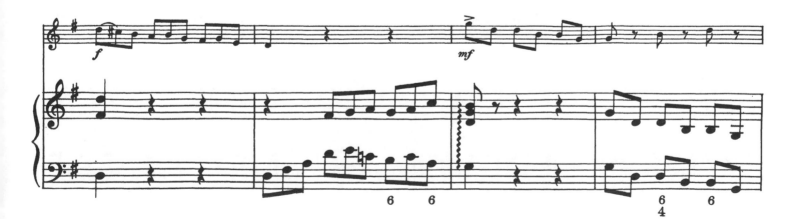

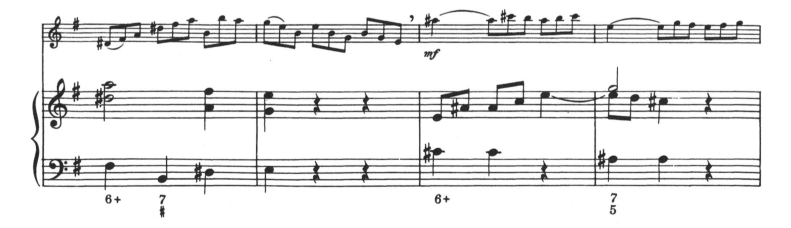

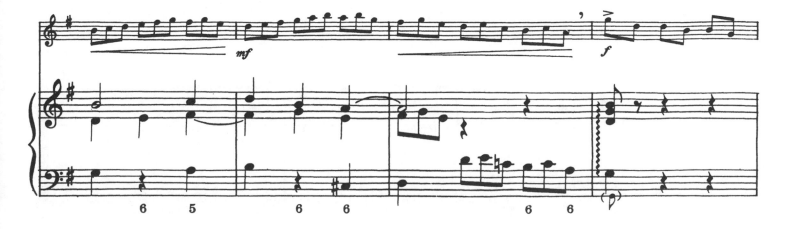

42805

Sonata in C minor
for Flute and Piano

From the *Methodischen Sonaten* (1732)

Georg Philipp Telemann (1681-1767)
Edited by Milton Wittgenstein
Figured bass realization by Thomas Wilt

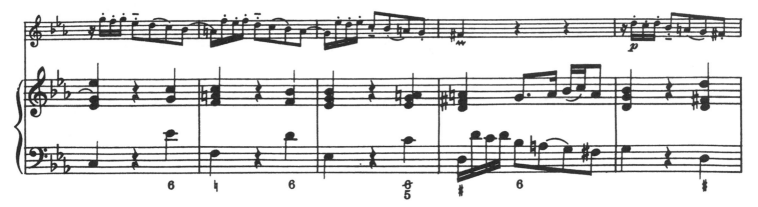

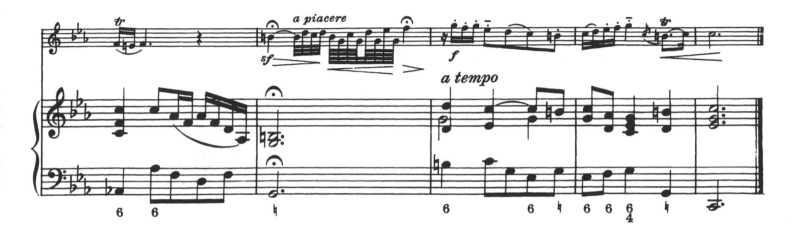

Allegro assai ♩ = 100

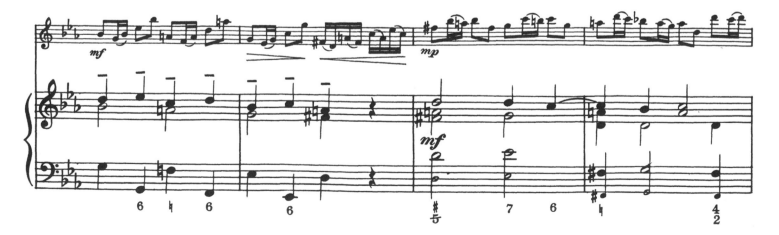

Ondeggiando, ma non adagio ♩=44

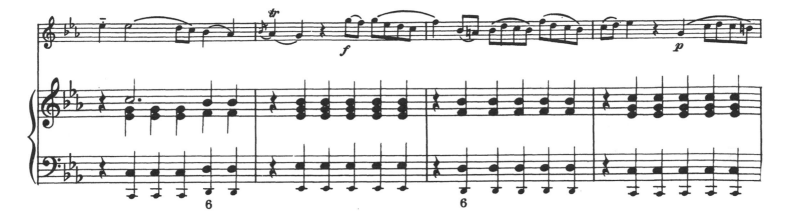

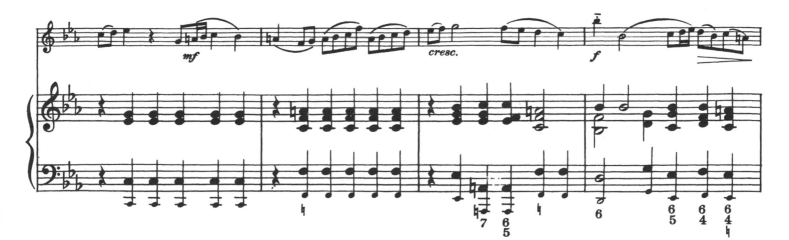

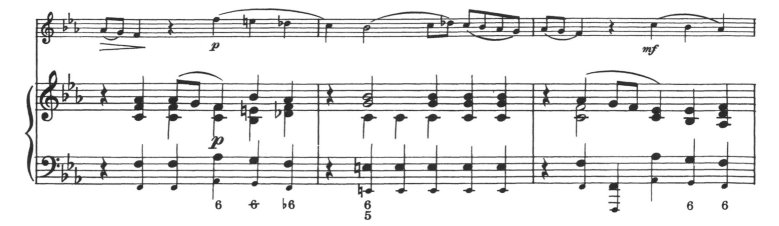

42805

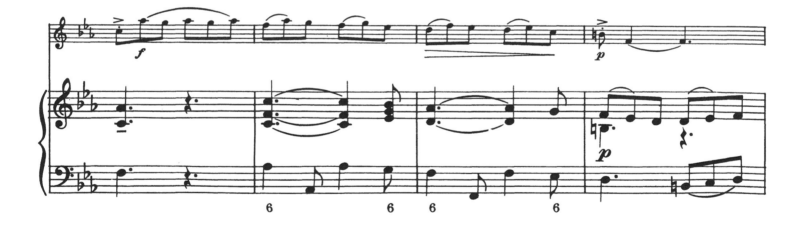

Sonata in F major
for Flute and Piano

From *Der Getreue Musikmeister* (1728)

Georg Philipp Telemann (1681-1767)
Edited by Milton Wittgenstein
Figured bass realization by Thomas Wilt

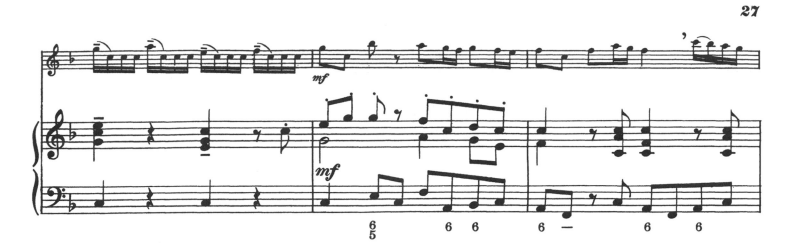

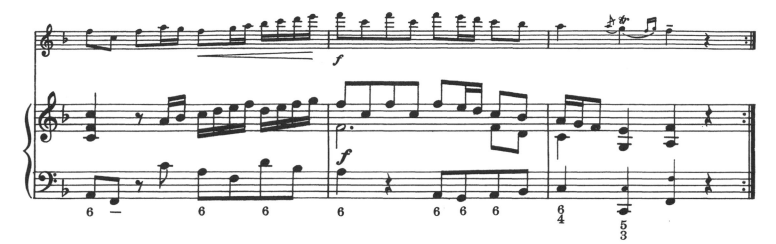

* The lower octave of the bass may be added throughout this movement

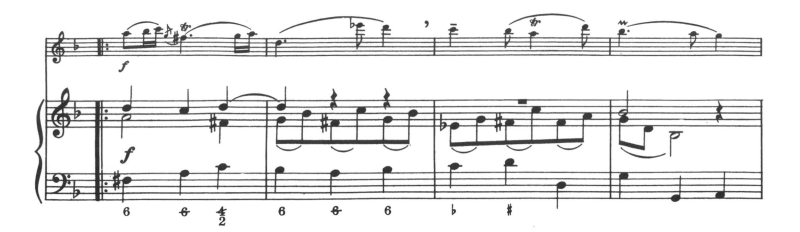

Georg Philipp Telemann

Four Sonatas

For Flute and Piano

Edited by

MILTON WITTGENSTEIN

Figured bass realization by

THOMAS WILT

G. SCHIRMER, Inc.

DISTRIBUTED BY

HAL•LEONARD®
CORPORATION
7777 W. BLUEMOUND RD. P.O. BOX 13819 MILWAUKEE, WI 53213

Sonata in G major
for Flute and Piano

Georg Philipp Telemann (1681-1767)
Edited by Milton Wittgenstein
Figured bass realization by Thomas Wilt

Flute

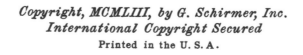

Flute

3

42805

4

Flute

Affettuoso ♪ = 76

Allegro ♩ = 138

senza rit.

Sonata in C minor
for Flute and Piano

Flute

From the *Methodischen Sonaten* (1732)

Georg Philipp Telemann (1681-1767)
Edited by Milton Wittgenstein
Figured bass realization by Thomas Wilt

42805

Flute

Allegro assai ♩ = 100

42805

Flute

Ondeggiando, ma non adagio ♩= 44

Sonata in F major
for Flute and Piano

Flute

Georg Philipp Telemann (1681-1767)
Edited by Milton Wittgenstein
Figured bass realization by Thomas Wilt

From *Der Getreue Musikmeister* (1728)

42805

Flute

Sonata in B♭ major
for Flute and Piano

Flute

Georg Philipp Telemann (1681-1767)
Edited by Milton Wittgenstein
Figured bass realization by Thomas Wilt

From the *Methodischen Sonaten* (1732)

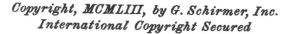

Allegro ♩=120

Flute

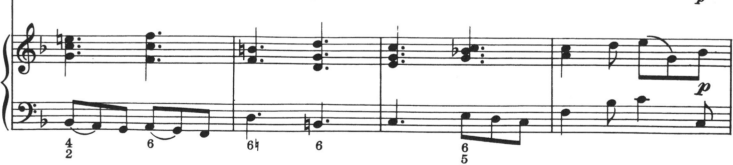

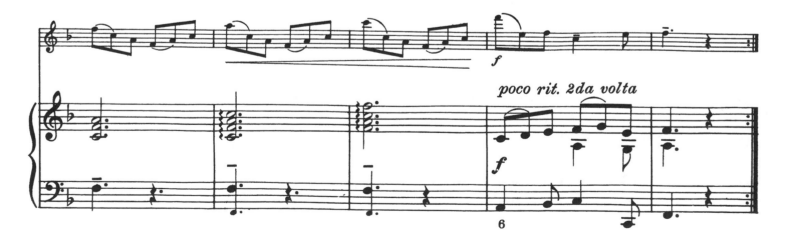

Sonata in B♭ major

for Flute and Piano

From the *Methodischen Sonaten* (1732)

Georg Philipp Telemann (1681-1767)
Edited by Milton Wittgenstein
Figured bass realization by Thomas Wilt

42805

Allegro ♩=120

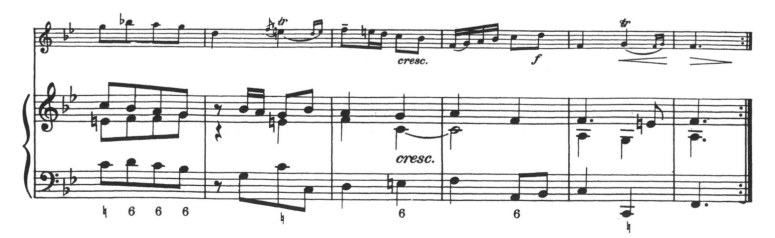

Allegretto ♪=120

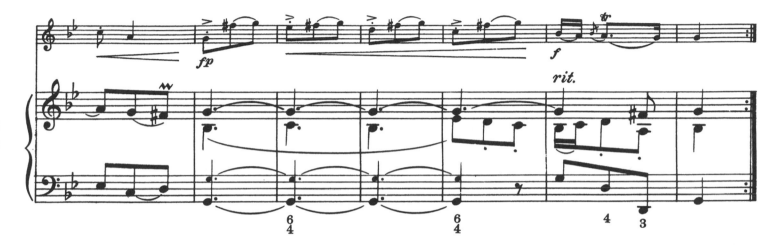

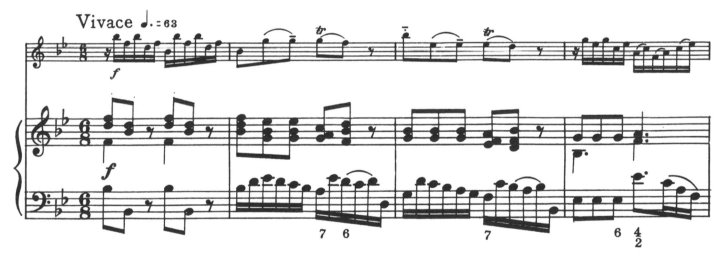

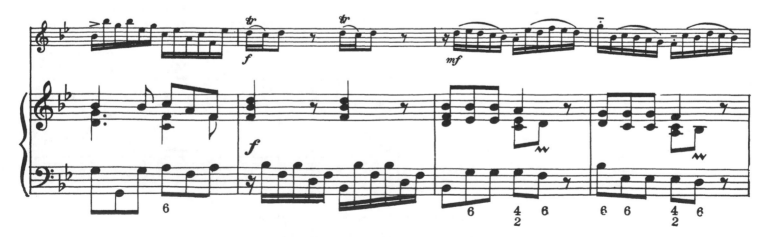

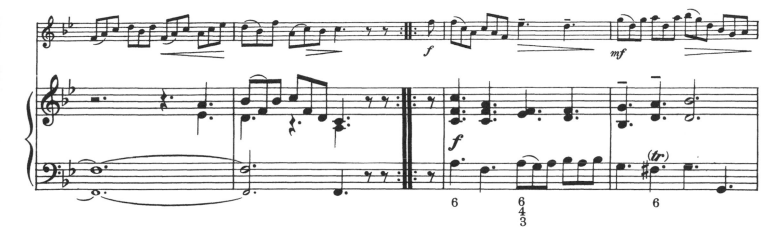